The Best Cartoons from
Leadership
Journal

Volume 3

"I like a pastor who makes things happen!"

The Best Cartoons from
Leadership
Journal
Volume 3

BROADMAN
&HOLMAN
PUBLISHERS

Nashville, Tennessee

©1999 by Christianity Today, Inc.
All rights reserved
Printed in the United States of America

Published by Broadman & Holman Publishers,
Nashville, Tennessee
Editorial Team: Leonard G. Goss, John Landers, Sandra Bryer

0-8054-1294-8

Dewey Decimal Classification: 817
Subject Heading: HUMOR

01 02 03 04 05 03 02 01 00 99

"It's the order of worship."

"So...if there are no more comments, we'll change the order of worship on Sunday."

Setting the Mood

Call to worship

Pastoral prayer

Special music

Bart's Scripture reading

"I tried to tell him not to change the order of service."

"All right, everyone synchronize your alarms. Joe, you at 12 noon. I'll do 12:01. Jeff, you're 12:02."

"I think we'd better buy smaller letters
and spell the word out."

"Welcome to our church—even though you're
sitting in our family pew..."

The whole church watched with nervous
anticipation as the visitors sat where the Martins
have sat for 42 years.

© 1983 Rob Portlock

"Clapping or nonclapping?"

SECTIONS

AMENS →

← HALLELUJAHS

PREACH IT, BROTHERS ↗

PORTLOCK

13

© 1982 Rob Portlock

"No, Pastor. It's spring forward, fall back."

14

"Welcome to our first dress-down Sunday."

15

"Welcome to our first early morning service."

Updating our Worship Language

Pastor Flebert finally discovers a way to
encourage promptness at worship.

"Well, that about wraps up the announcements—
whoa, wait a minute, I'm getting a fax
from the head usher right now."

19

"And for all members who never make the Sunday evening service, so you'll feel right at home, we're renaming it '60 Minutes.'"

"And now it's that time of our service for everyone
to stand, mingle, and schmooze."

©1992 Rob Portlock

PORTLOCK

"We have a special gift today for a lady who hasn't missed a service in 45 years. Eleanor Smith! Where is Eleanor sitting? Eleanor? Eleanor..."

"I hate football, but I love to be where people
are excited about something."

"I just love the way Dexter says 'Hallelujah!'"

"Frankly, I wasn't all that thrilled with applause, either."

"On the other hand, maybe we're not
ready for seeker services."

"I pray that this song I'm about to sing will not only
speak to your heart, but that it will spiritually
rip you limb from limb and lay you barren, naked,
and writhing in conviction on the cold, dank,
tile floor... Amen, God bless you."

"Relax, I'm only here for your Sunday evening service."

Associate minister Kevin "Good" Knievel, performs what would become known at First Church as his last stunt.

... and on the 7th day thou shalt clear the platform, check the sound system, replace the broken guitar string, change the microphone battery, select the chorus transparencies, prepare the chord sheets, replace the broken overhead projector lens, tune the piano, attach the new drum heads, lead 2 worship services.... and rest.

Robertson

"They're putting choruses in hymnbooks and projecting hymns onto the screen. It's getting so I can't remember what I'm not supposed to like!"

35

"Okay—we'll do the rock service, but forget about
rapping the Nicene Creed."

"Bernice, do you think when we sing the worship choruses you could play a bit more casually?"

"Oldies Night" at the contemporary church.

It suddenly occurred to Pastor Mike that contemporary music, which worked so well at a church he visited, might not be what was needed here.

"Everyone is really with her today."

"We're breaking in a new pianist."

41

WHEN A HYMN WRITER DAYDREAMS...

"We'll hear Pastor's points one and two, skip three, and conclude with point four."

"Sir, you have been recommended for our remedial singing class that meets in the basement of our annex."

"Okay, the only fair way to do it this morning is...
heads it's the hymnal, tails it's choruses."

Hymn #267 spawns an unexpected moon-walk
from Minister of Music Ronny Jiles.

"… and I got that scar from the chairman of the board during the second battle of 'Guitars in the Sanctuary' back in '71."

"If everyone would join us in the parlor, the pastor will lead us in a good old-fashioned hymn sing."

"No offense, Henry, but since I'll be preaching on 'Faith and the Nuclear Age,' maybe we should sing something other than 'Leaning on the Everlasting Arms.'"

"We'll sing the first verse, hum the second, and lip-sync the third."

50

Pastor Linquist can never hear "A Mighty Fortress Is Our God" without remembering his old youth group singing it to the tune of "Come on Baby, Light My Fire."

"Don't look now, but I think your worship leader is having a mid-service crisis."

One Unforgettable Hymn

"It's a memo from the board. They don't mind if you play the occasional hymn on your electric guitar; however, they'd rather you didn't play it with your teeth, set it on fire, or smash it at the end of your song."

"Couldn't we sing some faster hymns?"

From the horror film, "The Day of the Song Leader."

"And now, on verse three, all those who are balding join in with those who have a mole on their neck."

"I know we're trying not to be stuffy around here,
but let's not refer to 'A Mighty Fortress' as
'Martin Luther's Greatest Hit.'"

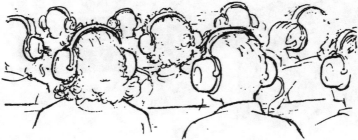

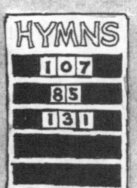

HYMNS
107
85
131

VEHICLES
WITH LIGHTS
LEFT ON
AFJ 87 D
71 LR 58

Sunday morning ... a small church in Philadelphia ...
they didn't think it could happen again!

"Something different today ...
live musicians and a taped soloist."

"For the choir's last number, we're really gonna
GET DOWN! Traditionally speaking, of course."

Church choir director Denzel Brainard knew
how to recruit choir participants.

"You can take only so much from a temperamental choir," thought Pastor Edwards as he waited to show the board a cost-saving idea.

Atomic alto Gladys Thundermuffin departs from the selection listed in the bulletin to do a solo interpretation of the Hallelujah Chorus.

"Retired chaplain. Wait till he calls
the choir to attention."

"Frankly, I haven't thought too much about the theology of the anthem. I figured I'd wait till we got the notes right."

"Me? I'm in here because I didn't put the CCLI numbers on my chorus sheets."

"Many thanks to the Ladies' Quilting Club
for the new choir robes."

71

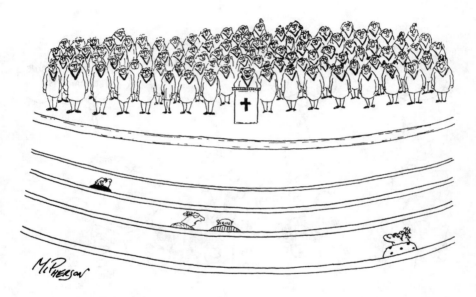

© 1989 John McPherson

"If you ask me, they got a little carried away with the choir membership drive."

"The sopranos and altos will sing 'Hallelujah,' the tenors will sing, 'Amen,' and the basses will sing 'Oo-wah, diddle-dee, doo-wah.'"

"Please disregard the music director's admonition to 'clap your hands, stomp your feet, and boogie till you drop' during the next hymn."

75

"Great seats, huh?"

"If you will fill out your temperature preference card and drop it in the offering plate, we will average them, and adjust the thermostat accordingly."

The celebrated roller-ushers of Third Church.

"To deal with the accusation that we at Cherry Hill Cathedral are culture bound, today's offertory hymn will be performed by the Duke Brothers."

© 1987 Ed Koehler

79

© 1988 Rob Portlock

Mrs. Riley forgets to check the volume control and catches Pastor Smith off guard.

© 1990 Nick Hobart

"Pianissimo."

"Did you know your pianist just played a Billy Joel tune as the offertory?"

"I don't care if his dad is chairman of the board; this is the last time he plays the offertory!"

As the offertory played on in all of its richness, energy, and syncopation, hardly anyone noticed that they were playing two different pieces.

"Roadcup, you've got a lot to learn about christening babies!"

"This is the pastor's first baptism."

"I left the baptistry running!"

"Do you have any with Nutra-Sweet™?"

"And now, we'll be blessed with a number
by the youth percussion ensemble."

"This song isn't really special to me, but it does provide a wonderful showcase for my voice."

© 1986 Mary Chambers

"I want to request prayer for my brother in the music ministry, Billy Lee Sanders, who was injured in a speaker avalanche last week."

"When we started using taped tracks,
I knew it wouldn't stop there."

PORTLOCK

The day Pastor Tim overcame his fear of telling those who couldn't sing, not to sing.

"Please tell me I didn't hear him say,
'Praise the Lord, oh Baby.'"

Lisa covers all the bases before she sings her solo

"Pastor just asked me to sing this morning ... I have a terrible sore throat ... My dog died this morning before—sniff—church ..."

"Don't ask the congregation to clap along.
They're rhythm-impaired."

Mrs. McNulty's ministry in song has changed somewhat since she started using "tracks."

Soloist Christine Kelly discovers that instead of background music she brought her tape by Z.Z. Top.

"The senior sermon is growing in popularity.
Last week only three came down."

"I want to thank Mrs. Smith and the drama team for that rousing drama presentation, and Stan ... that laser show was wonderful! Now, turn with me in your Bible for a brief word from our Sponsor."

"At this time, everyone over 12 is dismissed to go to Adults' Church in the basement."

"Oops! They forgot to clear the aisle before they dismissed the children for children's church!"

"I see our next speaker needs no introduction ..."

"Reverend Scottswell has become ill ...
Is there a doctoral candidate in the house?"

They may not remember Pastor Jones's sermons,
but his catchy theme song was unforgettable.

"And my hope is that our winless softball season has not affected us."

PORTLOCK

Though successful, Rev. Wheeler questions
the decision to start a puppet ministry.

© 1989 Lee Johnson

A.D. 43: Due to the increasing need for preaching,
the apostles turn the clown ministry over to the Seven.

"Looks like the pastor's lost control
of his congregation."

111

"If he finds nine points that spell S-U-P-E-R-B-O-W-L out of Genesis 22, he could become our all-time winner."

"This week I've decided to do unto you as you do unto me. Sit and stare all service."

"I trust your hearts are keenly focused
on what the Lord has to say to us this evening,
and not on the Lions' stinking loss to the Bears
this afternoon on that lousy holding penalty call
by the refs with 1:15 to go in the game!"

"Pastor Smith has invited you up here so he can have a chance just to stare at you!"

"And after my sermon, I'm sure you'll be interested in the picnic that's waiting for us right outside!"

The Wonder of Ministry

PORTLOCK

© 1984 Rob Portlock

119

"His eye is on the sparrow. Why, even the very, uh, blades of grass on your lawn are numbered."

"Yes. Yes. I see that hand."

"It has been said that the church today is too reliant upon psychology. How does that make you feel?"

"I think the deaf interpreter is ad-libbing again."

MCPHERSON

Pastor Dave Calhoun tries desperately
to make his sermons more lively.

The congregation always enjoyed it when Pastor Zumbach strayed a little from the pulpit...

...but just a little.

The Elvis Look-Alike Church

"Of course, the sermon illustration I've just given
is purely fictional and is not based upon
anyone here in the congregation."

"He'll be okay. He just married a couple
over at Devil's Run."

"Are you concentrating or just pretending?"

© 1997 Dan Pegoda

"And now if the ushers will collect all the bulletins, we will award the prize for best doodle of the day."

"Now, Mr. Remstedt, about these little drawings you do on the visitor information cards every Sunday ..."

You Know You're a Youth Pastor When ...

The only Sundays you preach are the
Fourth of July and Labor Day.

You Know You're a Youth Pastor When ...

Your office is any unused space in the church.

You Know You're a Youth Pastor When ...
Your idea of dressing up for church is wearing socks.

"He's good for another ten minutes at least."

OPTIMISTS FOR TODAY

Sets up all the folding chairs for Wednesday night Bible study!

Makes plans to meet his wife at 8:45 after an 8 o'clock board meeting!

Puts her shoes back on when the minister says "In conclusion..."!

140

"The trustees had it installed
after I ran past noon one time."

Calvary Church comes up with a solution
for sleeping-leg syndrome.

PASTOR JONES: GRADUATE OF THE FLIGHT ATTENDANT'S SCHOOL OF AFFABLE FAREWELLS

"B'bye. B'bye. So Long. Have a nice day. B'bye...."

"It was loud, forceful, and clashed with my sensibilities.
And that was just your tie."

"Well, that was fun. We must do it again sometime."

EXPRESS LINE
1 HELLO
1 HANDSHAKE
1 MINUTE CHIT CHAT

"... so my friend Marge said it might be phlebitis,
but when I asked the doctor, he said, 'Don't worry.
Just stay off your feet for a couple days,' but I told
him, 'Now how do you expect me to ...'"

The hotter the weather, the less First Church liked the
new naugahyde pew cushions.

"And we hope you'll join us after the service for… uh … uh … "

"If he goes over 30 seconds,
you get a free oil change."

152

153

© 1994 Steve Phelps

"Memorable candlelight service, Pastor."

"Uh, Erv, I understand you're the new chairman of the Worship Banner Committee."